Principles for a
Year-Round Winning Life

365 Daily Wisdom Nuggets

Principles for a
Year-Round Winning Life

365 Daily Wisdom Nuggets

EDITED BY: Titilola A. Akinyemi

PUBLISHED BY: Platform for Success Press
+1 917 826 3566, press@platformforsuccess.org

ORDERING INFORMATION:
To order this book, please write to:

Olu Ojeikere
121-12 Milburn Street,
Springfield Gardens, NY 11413
E-mail: Oluojeikere@yahoo.com

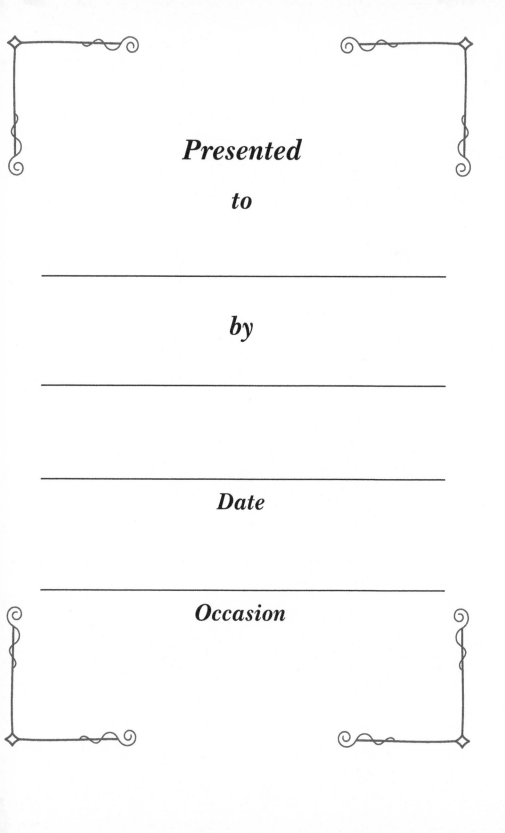

Presented

to

_____

by

_____

_____

Date

_____

Occasion

Contents

DEDICATION

I want to give thanks and praise to God, who sent His Son, Jesus Christ to die for me and transformed my life in remarkable ways. Without Him, I am nothing.

To my wife, Edna (aka Owell) and my two children, Esther and Daniel; the most significant relationships of my life: Thank you for loving me in spite of my shortcomings. Thank you for reminding me that regardless of our accomplishments, those who matter the most are the people who truly care.

To my siblings; Oluwole, Kolawole, Olayinka (aka Chairman), Oladele and Daisy (aka Efelomo): Each of you has deposited in me, the seed to do my best in all of my life endeavors. I am truly blessed to call you all family and I am forever grateful.

Olu Ojeikere

FOREWORD

Many focus on having a successful year, paying little or no attention to what they do on a daily basis. It takes a daily habit of victory to have a victorious year. These simple but impactful nuggets by Elder Olu Ojeikere have been carefully put together to impact your lives daily, for a triumphant year.

Dr. Festus Adeyeye
Senior Pastor
Abundant Life Christian Center Church
Brooklyn, New York.

INTRODUCTION

Have you ever seen a lawyer win a case in the court room without a thorough knowledge of the law? Similarly, to be successful across board, you must embrace the use of principles or wisdom nuggets, to guide your daily life. This book is designed to provide every reader with timeless principles that will enable you to face the challenges of life, and will help you to make wise decisions in many divergent situations.

JANUARY

JANUARY 1

We are not defined by the events that we experience in life; rather, it is the significance that we attribute to those events that have far reaching consequences in our lives.

Life Application: You have the choice to rise above or succumb to circumstances that you encounter in life; it is just a matter of your perspective.

JANUARY 2

Being confident of this very thing, that he which hath begun a good work in you will perform it until the day of Jesus Christ - Philippians 1:6 (KJV).

Life Application: Everyone on the planet desires successful outcomes in life. The truth is, every good thing has a starting point; and whatever God starts, He completes.

JANUARY 3

For I know the plans I have for you, says the Lord. They are plans for good and not for disaster, to give you a future and a hope - Jeremiah 29:11.

Life Application: I am yet to see a sane person that desires trouble for himself or herself. We are designed to seek good for ourselves. God has a good plan for our lives and that plan is to give us peace and to move us to our desired destinations, according to His will.

JANUARY 4

Ye are of God, little children, and have overcome them; because greater is He who is in you than he who is in the world - 1 John 4:5 (NASB).

Life Application: For those familiar with the 12-steps to addiction recovery, you know that without "a power greater than oneself," you cannot overcome the demon of addiction. We need a greater power to overcome the obstacles of life, and that greater power and person is Jesus Christ.

JANUARY 5

God's ability on your dis-ability will dis-able every attack of the enemy.

Life Application: The enemy always attacks you at the level of your disability, but when you reach out for God's ability, you become an overcomer.

JANUARY 6

If you know who you are and whose you are, you will not fear the outcome of a thousand battles.

Life Application: One of the weapons that the enemy uses, is to attack your identity. If the enemy can convince you to question your identity, he has defeated you. Know who and whose you are.

JANUARY 7

Favor is not fair, but it is a divine instrument that God uses to bring flavor into your life.

Life Application: There is no doubt that God knows that life is not fair; hence, He uses the instrument of favor as a leveler or a buffer, to give you an added advantage.

JANUARY 8

The greatest need of the entire human race is the transformation of the heart.

Life Application: We use legislation to change human affairs, and conditions, to build modern society; but we cannot use legislation to change the hearts of men. The love of God is the key for the transformation of the heart.

JANUARY 9

Do not neglect the daily reading of God's word; a day missed is transformation delayed.

Life Application: A consistent application of knowledge makes a student skillful in school. A consistent application of the knowledge derived from the reading of God's words, makes us skillful in the school of life.

JANUARY 10

The love of God is greater than the darkness of your past and present. Remember ye not the former things, neither consider the things of old, for I will do a new thing - Isaiah 43:18-19 (KJV).

Life Application: Many people are depressed because of the failures of their past and inadequacies of their present. However, the love of God gives us a reason to live a life of liberty without owing anyone an apology.

JANUARY 11

Do what you can, with what you have, where you are – Anonymous.

Life Application: Do not wait for everything to be in place before making a godly move. Progress is made with every step you take to accomplish your desired goal.

JANUARY 12

Until you decide to grow, you will continue to groan.

Life Application: Every parent will agree that when a newborn baby is not showing signs of growth, there are bound to be concerns. Growth is nature's expectation and it is applicable in every area of our lives. When we are not growing, we are dying.

JANUARY 13

Finish each day before you begin the next, and interpose a solid wall of sleep between the two. This you cannot do without temperance - Ralph Waldo Emerson.

Life Application: One of the secrets of successful people is starting every day with a plan and reflecting on that day's accomplishment, rather than procrastinating always, and desiring to accomplish things "in the future."

JANUARY 14

Just for today, choose to be pleasantly productive.

Life Application: You can do one of three things daily: Invest in each day, waste each day, or spend each day. The choice is yours.

JANUARY 15

The secret of your success is determined by your daily agenda - John Maxwell.

Life Application: You are either waking up every day with a plan to succeed or with a plan to fail. Success is not incidental; it requires a conscious effort.

JANUARY 16

You will never change your life until you change something you do daily - John Maxwell.

Life Application: I am not opposed to self-help books; however, what good are self-help books if the individual is not willing to make personal changes in his or her daily routines?

JANUARY 17

There is a time when we must firmly choose the course we will follow or, the relentless drifts of events will make the decision for us - Herbert V. Prochnow.

Life Application: I have learned from personal experience and great people that having the power to decide is not enough; there must be a corresponding determination to follow through. Decision and determination lead to successful outcomes.

JANUARY 18

Stand fast therefore in the liberty wherewith Christ hath made us free, and be not entangled again with the yoke of bondage - Galatians 5:1-2 (KJV).

Life Application: "I am free," is not a right but a privilege. With that privilege comes responsibility and accountability. This applies to all facets of life.

JANUARY 19

As Arthur L. Williams entitled his book, "All you can do is all you can do; but all you can do is enough."

Life Application: In life, there is always the question of "What is one's potential?" You cannot realize your potential until you apply yourself to doing all that you are created for. Your readiness to apply yourself to a given task reveals your potential.

JANUARY 20

Do not settle for the permissible; reach out for greatness.

Life Application: It is easier to make excuses and accomplish little, rather than to inconvenience oneself to move higher and do better in life.

JANUARY 21

Try to leave an environment better than how you met it.

Life Application: Personal Reflections: Have you ever asked yourself why some people are welcomed with open arms in organizations where they previously worked, while the mention of other previous employees' names invokes negative comments? The simple answer is the value that they brought to those organizations.

JANUARY 22

He gives strength to the weary and increases the power of the weak - Isaiah 40:29 (NIV).

Life Application: When all hope is gone, God gives you the strength to continue and the determination to be unrelenting in your efforts.

JANUARY 23

It is God who worketh in you both to will and to do of his good pleasure - Philippians 2:13 (KJV).

Life Application: While man is a free-will being and can choose good or evil, it takes a God-directed person to do good.

JANUARY 24

Significance is found in the hearts and lives of those who live beyond themselves/for others.

Life Application: More attention is drawn to you, when you are successful; however, you become significant only when you start impacting lives.

JANUARY 25

You say, "I am allowed to do anything," - but not everything is good for you. You say, "I am allowed to do anything," - but not everything is beneficial - 1 Corinthians 10:23.

Life Application: In a world filled with many choices, only the wise person understands these two facts; there is the power to choose, and there is the power to know and choose what is right and beneficial.

JANUARY 26

When you can do the common things of life in an uncommon way, you will command the attention of the world - George Washington Carver.

Life Application: There is recognition when one mixes the creative with the monotonous, resulting in an extraordinary feat.

JANUARY 27

Success is when preparation meets with opportunity.

Life Application: Opportunities come to everyone, but only the person that is prepared makes good use of such opportunities. Be prepared, in and out of season.

JANUARY 28

God does not provide us with equal distribution of wealth; rather, He provides us with opportunities.

Life Application: Some people are quick to blame God or others for poverty in the world; yet very few remember to give credit to God for the opportunities that He gives us, which are based upon our talents and readiness to act on those opportunities.

JANUARY 29

Your determination to succeed in life must be greater than the opposition against you - Dr. Festus Adeyeye.

Life Application: In the path of success, there are obstacles, and your resolve to overcome them must be greater than the obstacles themselves.

JANUARY 30

Just Do It! Do not postpone until tomorrow, what you should do today.

Life Application: Procrastination is a thief of time and opportunity. I learned that firsthand while writing this very book. Shun procrastination.

JANUARY 31

Do not give up; try, try, and try again!

Life Application: Keep on trying, because in the long run, only those who made attempts will succeed.

FEBRUARY

FEBRUARY 1

It is impossible to worship the empty promises of this world and still make God your number one priority - Pete Wilson.

Life Application: Have you ever heard about competing values? It is having multiple choices; however, only one, God, can set you free.

FEBRUARY 2

Forgiveness says you are given another chance to make a new beginning - Joan Gattuso.

Life Application: This is an eternal truth; forgiveness is allowing yourself to be divine.

FEBRUARY 3

Your greatest temptation in life will not be to chase after what is obviously evil, but rather, what is deceptively good.

Life Application: Many will frown at stealing, but many will embrace complacency directly or indirectly. Yet, the rate of detriment from complacency is far more rapid. Be spiritually alert to tell the difference between "good" and "deceptively good."

FEBRUARY 4

Free to live! Free to love! Free to be me! How do you attain such a level of freedom?

Life Application: Freedom is found in Jesus Christ. There is only one way to find relief from crippling approval addiction; relief is found in the unconditional love and acceptance of our Lord and Savior, Jesus Christ.

FEBRUARY 5

All for one and one for all; this is the secret of every truly great family.

Life Application: It is the secret of "we-ness" not "me-ness," that makes families to flourish.

FEBRUARY 6

For with God, nothing shall be impossible - Mark 1:37 (KJV).

Life Application: Of a truth, no matter the resources available to us as human beings, they are limited, compared to the limitless resources God can provide.

FEBRUARY 7

The strength of your enemy is your ignorance.

Life Application: You learn this truth in your dealings with people; you pay dearly for what you do not know.

FEBRUARY 8

Our life situation falls into one of three categories: We are either coming out of a crisis, in the middle of a crisis, or about to walk into a crisis.

Life Application: No one is immune from the crises of life, but the key to overcoming crises in life, is one's ability to navigate through and prevail.

FEBRUARY 9

An eternal perspective can change everything. It can help you to make sense of the situation that you are passing through right now.

Life Application: You are familiar with the phrase "the bigger picture." Yes, when you see the bigger picture, you understand the situation better and become well-equipped to deal with it.

FEBRUARY 10

Life on earth is important, but there is more than this world can offer; we are made for eternity.

Life Application: Life is for the living, yet some die hoping for a better life. It is called eternity essence.

FEBRUARY 11

If I find in myself a desire which no experience in this world can satisfy, the most probable explanation is that I was made for another world - C.S. Lewis.

Life Application: We have many people feeling empty on the inside, yet they want "more." When I hear people say that they want "more," my response to them is simply, "more for what?" Can you identify what you really need?

FEBRUARY 12

For Christians, eternity does not begin when we die, but right now, as we choose to live in Christ.

Life Application: Many of us fall into the erroneous belief that being a Christian is waiting for something good to happen at eternity; whereas, the opposite is the case; experiencing goodness is part of an ongoing God-kind of life, here on earth.

FEBRUARY 13

Tell me what you have, and I will tell you who you are – Author Unknown.

Life Application: My daily interactions with people have led me to this fundamental truth: An unwise person speaks out from lack of wisdom, while a wise person speaks from the depth of wisdom. In all your getting, get wisdom.

FEBRUARY 14

Love takes off masks that we fear we cannot live without and know we cannot live within - James Baldwin.

Life Application: Genuine love accepts us for who we are and does not leave us where we are.

FEBRUARY 15

Situations in life may not ever change or get better, but with Jesus, you improve.

Life Application: No matter the effort we expend to make our lives better, the truth is, outside of Jesus, we are at best described as miserable.

FEBRUARY 16

My grace is sufficient for you; for my strength is made perfect in your weakness - 2 Cor. 12:9 (NKJV).

Life Application: When the doctor says it is over, and asks you to go home and await death, all seems hopeless; but God gives us strength to believe in the miraculous.

FEBRUARY 17

You can only overcome something you refuse to tolerate.

Life Application: There is always something in us that tolerates a negative, addictive behavior. Having the right support is good, but having the courage to confront the behavior is better.

FEBRUARY 18

Success comes when you do what you love to do and commit to be the best in your field – Brian Tracey.

Life Application: Doing the right thing with the right attitude and focused determination gets you the desired results in life. Always remember this fact; success is not an accident waiting to happen.

FEBRUARY 19

Your vision gets larger as you grow; your vision does not move until you move - John Maxwell.

Life Application: No matter how well intentioned one's vision is, it will not produce any results, unless one acts upon the vision.

FEBRUARY 20

Your confession will either imprison you or set you free.

Life Application: You become what you confess. Your confession has the potential to chart a desired course of life.

FEBRUARY 21

Passion is essential for success.

Life Application: Show me an individual that has succeeded in any endeavor in life, and I will show you an individual who is passionate about what he or she does.

FEBRUARY 22

A person who never made a mistake, never tried anything new - Albert Einstein.

Life Application: You must understand that "mistake" is not such a bad word after all. It just means that one misses the target at the first attempt.

FEBRUARY 23

Focus is the strength and secret of a successful person.

Life Application: Every book that I have read about successful people expresses one common trait among them; their determination to turn every setback into a comeback.

FEBRUARY 24

Until you perspire to inspire, you will never aspire to any human endeavor.

Life Application: The difference between a successful person and an unsuccessful person is the desire to give all it requires to accomplish a task.

FEBRUARY 25

We are Christ's ambassadors. God is using us to speak to you; we beg you as though Christ Himself were here pleading with you, receive the love He offers -be reconciled to God - 2 Cor. 5:20 (TLB).

Life Application: I will rather be a carrier of good news than an agent of doom.

FEBRUARY 26

God is not nearly as concerned with your ability, as He is with your surrender.

Life Application: A careful study of the men and women that God used in the Bible shows that God uses people that are broken and receptive to His divine purposes.

FEBRUARY 27

Every trial I face is altered by God for my ultimate good.

Life Application: One of the ironies of life is that many want to experience victory in life, but only few appreciate the necessity of trials on the road to victory.

FEBRUARY 28

Trials are not meant to steal your joy; rather, they are designed as stepping-stones to your next level.

Life Application: Wrapped in every trial is an opportunity for better things. Your perspective makes the difference.

MARCH

MARCH 1

Whatever we value reveals the state of our hearts.

Life Application: Our outward disposition is determined by our inner beliefs.

MARCH 2

Character is not made in a crisis; it is only exhibited - Robert Freeman.

Life Application: Our true character is revealed in our unguarded moments.

MARCH 3

A faithful man will abound with blessings; but he who hastens to be rich will not go unpunished - Proverbs 28:20 (KJV).

Life Application: One of the keys to success in life is doing the right thing every time and everywhere, continuously.

MARCH 4

A fool vents all his feelings, but a wise man holds them back - Proverbs 29:11 [NKJV].

Life Application: I have the right to express my feelings, but I also have the power to regulate my feelings and not allow them to get the best of me.

MARCH 5

God is good all the time, and all the time He is good; even in your situation, right now.

Life Application: It is difficult for the human mind to comprehend that even on our worst days, God still has a plan for us.

MARCH 6

Think like a person of action. Act like a person of thought.

Life Application: I think, I act. Both go together; otherwise you are a dead man.

MARCH 7

Where you are today is largely the result of the decision you made yesterday. Where you will be tomorrow is largely based on the decision you are making right now.

Life Application: Nothing is accidental in life, and thus, decisions are very important. You are always making decisions whether big or small. Decide wisely.

MARCH 8

You are not the victim of the circumstances that you experience; rather, you are the maker of the decisions that can work for you.

Life Application: Circumstances are life events that we have no control over, but how we respond to them is totally within our control.

MARCH 9

Never put off until tomorrow, what you can do the day after tomorrow – Mark Twain.

Life Application: Actually, procrastination is a thief of time. Start making the changes you want to see, right now.

MARCH 10

But the Lord is faithful, and He will strengthen and protect you from the evil one - 2 Thessalonians 3:3 [NASB].

Life Application: We take insurance against adverse events, but we have assurance when we depend on God's provisions.

MARCH 11

Simplified living is about more than doing less; it is being who God called you to be.

Life Application: Live your life purposefully without creating additional complications for yourself.

MARCH 12

The only God it makes sense to entrust ourselves to, is the God of the Bible.

Life Application: This is not being religious or shortsighted. The fact is that other gods are displayed on wooden and carved images, but the God of the Bible lives inside of anyone that invites Him in.

MARCH 13

The joy Jesus gives is not grounded in our circumstances; it is grounded in Him.

Life Application: Happiness is dependent on your life circumstances, but joy is having a deep conviction that everything will be alright.

MARCH 14

A mistake is not wasted if you can learn from it.

Life Application: A person who has never made a mistake is either a beast or a god. Let your mistakes serve as learning tools.

MARCH 15

Each day brings new opportunities to learn and grow. Embrace the new you, every day.

Life Application: Only the unwise live each day without learning something new.

MARCH 16

God gives us wonderful blessings and joy, but it is okay to want more of Him.

Life Application: God's blessings are not a substitute for His presence.

MARCH 17

Gratitude is never wasted, and a thankful person is rarely depressed. Be thankful for life today.

Life Application: Gratitude is contagious because it impacts everyone around you.

MARCH 18

Trust men, and they will be true to you; trust them greatly, and they will show themselves great - Ralph Waldo Emerson.

Life Application: To be trusted, trust others.

MARCH 19

The measure of your life will not be in what you accumulated, but in what you gave away - Dr. Wayne Dyer.

Life Application: Your life is enlarged by the degree to which you are willing to give to others.

MARCH 20

To believe in something and not to live it is dishonest - Mahatma Gandhi.

Life Application: It must be draining to expend energy and time trying to be something that you are not. Live your truth.

MARCH 21

Every good intention will always attract opposition.

Life Application: Since some people are comfortable with the status quo, they misconstrue every good change as a threat.

MARCH 22

Attempt something great today.

Life Application: Every day has its share of ups and downs. Nevertheless, always look for opportunities to make a change.

MARCH 23

True friendship is known in times of adversity.

Life Application: Whenever I do a quick five-minute assessment on people experiencing difficulties in life, I always find a missing link - the lack of true friends.

MARCH 24

You cannot give up; God is not finished yet.

Life Application: Your decision not to give up is your express permission that God needs, to help you.

MARCH 25

If your vision does not scare you, it is too small - Matt Batterson.

Life Application: Some people pursue small visions because they think the idea of a big vision is a license for failure.

MARCH 26

Grace and Mercy are unearned blessings.

Life Application: There is no one that has ever worked to deserve mercy and grace. It is a divine providence to compensate for man's shortcomings.

MARCH 27

Be a purpose-driven person and not a reactive-driven person.

Life Application: Every time I am confronted with challenges, one thing defines my response - "I am a person of being."

MARCH 28

The mind is framed by what it takes in - Will Durant.

Life Application: In the absence of the Spirit of God, your life is a sum of what your mind has acquired.

MARCH 29

God's love stands when everything else fails.

Life Application: The most powerful force in the world is love. That love is not found in anyone but in God, because it has the power to change lives and restore hope to the broken-hearted.

MARCH 30

Even in your worst-case scenario, God still has a beautiful plan for your life.

Life Application: My life circumstances do not alter God's plans for me.

MARCH 31

What you behold daily is what you ultimately become.

Life Application: Sometimes you wonder why some people are shocked at what they have become. However, they fail to ask themselves what their objects of attention or attraction have been.

APRIL

APRIL 1

Focus on what is in front of you; worry less about what is coming down the road.

Life Application: Many of us rob ourselves of the blessings of now; instead, we create anxiety about future events that we have no control over.

APRIL 2

Being hopeful is one of the keys to a graceful life.

Life Application: There is a better you and a better tomorrow waiting to emerge. If you do not believe it, you will end up being frustrated with life.

APRIL 3

Sometimes, you need to burn bridges to stop yourself from crossing them again - Toby McKeehan.

Life Application: "Do not burn bridges" is a popular saying. However, I had the personal experience of burning some bridges to get to where I am in my career today. Not all bridges lead you to your desired destination.

APRIL 4

God can re-make what is broken.

Life Application: Life is filled with broken people, and only God, not human legislation, identifies the root of our brokenness; He also has the power to heal broken people.

APRIL 5

If any would be great among you, let him serve others – A paraphrase of Jesus' words to his disciples.

Life Application: The service we extend to others is an invitation to greatness for us.

APRIL 6

But He was wounded for our transgressions, He was bruised for our iniquities; The chastisement for our peace was upon Him, And by His stripes we are healed - Isaiah 53:5 (NKJV).

Life Application: Faith obtains what Grace has made available. If we believe God's promises, everything that Jesus' death provided becomes yours.

APRIL 7

Rejoice, again I say, Rejoice!

Life Application: "Rejoice," is as much a command as "Repent" - Andrew Bonar.

APRIL 8

For I know the thoughts that I think towards you, says the Lord, thoughts of peace and not of evil, to give you a future and a hope – Jeremiah 29:11 (NKJV).

Life Application: God may not grant you all you desire; but He will grant you what you need. Trust Him; His ways are the best.

APRIL 9

Life is partly what we make it and partly what it is made by the friends we choose - Tennessee William.

Life Application: You are like a sponge that soaks up liquid - any type of liquid. You become, based on association and decision. Choose sensibly.

APRIL 10

Everything that irritates us about others can lead us to an understanding of ourselves - Carl Jung.

Life Application: I have found the secret to having lesser arguments with people. How, you may ask? By being true to myself and understanding how I react to situations. As such, before people's words and actions affect you negatively, ask yourself these questions: "How do I feel now?" "What would I do in this person's shoes?" Then, choose your words wisely.

APRIL 11

Loving people live in a loving world; hostile people live in a hostile world. Same world - Wayne Dyer.

Life Application: You become what you make of your world.

APRIL 12

Forgiveness does not change the past, but it does change the future - Paul Boose.

Life Application: A lot of movies show us how satisfying revenge can be, but they never detail the hell people go through, when they are unforgiving. The headache. The weight loss. The nightmares. The sleepless nights. When you are unforgiving, you let people live rent free in your head. You must forgive others, for your own wellbeing.

APRIL 13

The key to long term success is a willingness to disrupt your own comfort for the sake of continued growth - Todd Henry.

Life Application: Do not allow yesterday's success to stop your motivation for continuous success in life.

APRIL 14

There hath no temptation taken you but such as man can bear; But God is faithful, who will not suffer you to be tempted above what you are able; but will with every temptation make also the way of escape that you may be able to endure it - 1 Cor. 10:13 (ASV).

Life Application: Temptations are commonplace in life, but God expects us to engage our willpower. The wise person should know that he or she has - and must engage - will power, to overcome temptations.

APRIL 15

But let none of you suffer as a murderer, a thief, an evildoer, or as a busybody in other people's matters – 1 Peter 4:15 (NIV).

Life Application: Do not let other people's business put you into a personal crisis.

APRIL 16

Celebrate the joy of living today and pray for the uncertainty of tomorrow.

Life Application: Look back on all the times you have ever worried about anything. You are still alive, and all is well. If you survived before, you can and will survive again.

APRIL 17

A good name is the greatest investment you can give your family and your generation.

Life Application: Doing what is right matters a great deal, even if it is in what seems to be the smallest of matters.

APRIL 18

Strength does not come from winning. Rather, your struggles develop your strengths. Strength is when you go through hardships and decide not to surrender.

Life Application: Life can be hard, sometimes. My advice? "Endure hardship well."

APRIL 19

The mind is formed by what it takes in - Will Durant.

Life Application: Whatever you listen to, whomever you spend time with, wherever you stay, is a sum total of who you become. Guard your eyes and ears all the time, as they are the gateways to your mind.

APRIL 20

"Speak Life, speak Life,
To the deadest darkest night; Speak Life, speak life,
When the sun won't shine, and you don't know why; Look into the eyes of the broken hearted,
Watch them come alive as soon as you speak hope;
You speak love..." - Lyrics from Toby Mac's Song, "Speak Life."

Life Application: Kind words can lift a heavy heart.

APRIL 21:

Now faith is confidence in what we hope for and assurance about what we do not see - Hebrews 11:1 (NIV).

Life Application: We have to walk by faith, to possess all that is duly ours - Lailah Gifty Akita.

APRIL 22

Miracles are not accidents; miracles happen in the lives of people who make room for God to do great things in their lives.

Life Application: Miracles happen every day; do not stop believing.

APRIL 23

Faith as small as a mustard seed can move mountains – Matthew 17:20.

Life Application: When you are out of resources, just take what you have and place them in God's hands. God does a lot with a little.

APRIL 24

The enemy wants to trick you into falling into debt, but God's promise for you is abundance. Take charge of your finances.

Life Application: Sometimes, all you need to do is to say "No," to save yourself from the heartache of financial debt. Learn to understand delayed gratification.

APRIL 25

It is easy to waste time and energy on superficial relationships with artificial people.

Life Application: If a relationship, association, or venture is taking more than you are giving from you, cut it off.

APRIL 26

Give attention to what is in your hands and not what is in someone else's hands.

Life Application: Focus on you; focus on growing; focus on being better; and you will be glad you did.

APRIL 27

For I reckon that the sufferings of this present time are not worthy to be compared with the glory that shall be revealed in us - Romans 8:18 (KJV).

Life Application: God is forming you for your future. Every test and trial is preparing you for your purpose. Embrace the process.

APRIL 28

Nobody gets to live life backward. Look ahead; that is where your future lies - Ann Landers.

Life Application: Life is for the living, not for waiting and wandering around.

APRIL 29

Starting is a choice. If fear is the only thing keeping you from your future, then it is time to shake yourself free.

Life Application: Do it afraid. Learn along the way, you will be just fine.

APRIL 30

For every irritation, God has some inspiration. Learn to take the best out of the worst situations of life - Dee Lamp.

Life Application: God's got you; never forget that.

MAY

MAY 1

When there is war, there is a way; when there is a will; there is an action - Levi Lusko.

Life Application: Do not give up.

MAY 2

If you hear a voice within you that says you cannot paint, then by all means paint, and that voice will be silenced - Vincent Willem van Gogh.

Life Application: Sometimes your biggest enemy is your "Inner man." Do not let your own doubts defeat your God-given destiny.

MAY 3

When you think positively, good things happen.

Life Application: Imagine and expect good things to happen to you today.

MAY 4

Opinions are cheap, and cheap things never last.

Life Application: Do not allow people's opinions to hinder your uniqueness.

MAY 5

Some people are real; some people are good; some people are fake; and some people are really good at being fake – Author Unknown.

Life Application: Always focus on people's motives, rather than on their external presentations.

MAY 6

We live in a world where bad is good and good is bad. If you have the spirit of God in you and you know it is right, then do it.

Life Application: Owe no one an apology for doing what is right.

MAY 7

Because the foolishness of God is wiser than men and the weakness of God is stronger than men - 1 Cor. 1:25 (NKJV).

Life Application: God always makes sense out of supposedly dumb matters.

MAY 8

And I am certain that God, who began the good work within you, will continue his work until it is finally finished on the day when Christ Jesus returns – Philippians 1:6.

Life Application: Hold on to God's promises. Your future is bigger and better than your past experiences.

MAY 9

Whatever it takes to make it, I am going all the way; I may be down sometimes; I will not be down always - Lyrics by Sounds of Blackness.

Life Application: The greatness of a man is not in succeeding; it is in what he does after he has fallen.

MAY 10

A double-minded man is unstable in all of his ways - James 1:8 (KJV).

Life Application: There is something about being indecisive. It makes you lose all the time; not just in the place of prayer, but in life. Learn to make a decision, and stand by it always.

MAY 11

Consider it pure joy my brothers and sisters whenever you face trials of many kinds - James 1:2 (NIV).

Life Application: When managed properly, trials are seeds for our next level of success.

MAY 12

How you do anything is how you will do everything.

Life Application: Always maintain a position of excellence in all that you do.

MAY 13

Step out in faith; do not wait and waste time.

Life Application: Big dreams can be really scary. However, the more you delay, the more time passes, and one day you would wake up and see your dream in another person's hand.

MAY 14

Make a deliberate decision to move from the realm of fear to the realm of faith.

Life Application: Fear and faith are opposite sides of a coin. They cannot coexist, so one has to go. You cannot serve two masters at the same time.

MAY 15

Do not allow what you cannot do to stop what God can do.

Life Application: Do not forget the part of the scripture that says, "With God all things are possible."

MAY 16

When you are faced with a difficult situation, just do the right thing.

Life Application: Two wrongs can never make a right.

MAY 17

God sends no one away empty, except those who are full of themselves - D.L Moody.

Life Application: Approach God as a man without options; as a man who seeks His will.

MAY 18

Come to me, all you who are weary and burdened, and I will give you rest. Matthew 11:28 (NIV).

Life Application: Only a God-filled life brings a joy-full life.

MAY 19

Where God guides, He provides.

Life Application: One factor that determines if you are doing God's will is that there is always provision for everything. When he leads, do follow.

MAY 20

Money is the reward for solving problems for others - Mike Murdock.

Life Application: A lot of people focus on being rich and wealthy, failing to understand that you get paid for the value you offer. From today, give value.

MAY 21

A bad attitude is like a flat tire; until you change it, you are going nowhere - Author Unknown.

Life Application: People bless you and take you to the next level of your life based on how you make them feel. Attitude is everything.

MAY 22

Every human disappointment can become a divine appointment.

Life Application: All things, whether good or bad, work together for your good. Maintain this mindset.

MAY 23

Divine encounters always produce manifestations beyond our expectations.

Life Application: Only one word from God about a particular situation, changes everything. Seek to hear God's will.

MAY 24

Do not allow temporary disappointments to waste your talents.

Life Application: Disappointments are bound to happen, but the rule of the game is to stand up, dust yourself, improvise, and move on. You've got this!

MAY 25

When the celebration of sin replaces the confession of sin, God removes His presence. Saying, "God bless me," does not bring Him back.

Life Application: God hates sin; you cannot change His mind about it.

MAY 26

Pressure is feeling the push of culture to stray from our faith. Persecution, is feeling the pain of the choices made, as we stand for our faith.

Life Application: Our society has that tendency to subtly put you under pressure. To live above pressure, you need to believe God's word as though it is all you will ever need to survive.

MAY 27

The matter that you think makes your anger, "righteous," is the very issue you are called to forgive.

Life Application: One of the things I have learned about anger and forgiveness is patience. When you get really angry about someone's flaws, stop, and ask yourself; "What if I were the one with the flaws, would I wish to be forgiven?"

MAY 28

A crowded heart is an enemy of a fruitful life - Levi Lusko

Life Application: Bitterness and jealousy are like heavy baggage that prevent you from being fruitful and productive. Watch out for the little foxes!

MAY 29

Do not be quickly provoked in your spirit, for anger resides in the lap of fools – Eccl. 7:9 (NIV).

Life Application: Learn to forgive an offence before it even happens. Every man has flaws that would tend to provoke you to anger.

MAY 30

Forfeiting our right to anger makes us deny ourselves and makes us others-centered - Brant Hansen.

Life Application: In place of anger, choose long-suffering and patience.

MAY 31

When you are looking for more, you are missing out on what you have and who you are with - Levi Lusko.

Life Application: To be satisfied and content is a virtue you need if you want to enjoy your life.

JUNE

JUNE 1

Be alert and of sober mind. Your enemy the devil prowls around like a roaring lion looking for someone to devour - 1 Peter 5:8 (NIV).

Life Application: The devil does not have to talk you out of anything; he just needs to talk you into doing more things that will destroy you.

JUNE 2

God is love.

Life Application: Love is more than what we see in movies and books. Love as God wants it to be, is when we put others before us. It is something that human nature finds hard to achieve; but with God, love is easy.

JUNE 3

So that the proof of your faith being more precious than gold, which is perishable, even though tested by fire, may be found to result in praise and glory and honor at the revelation of Jesus – 1 Peter 1:7 (NASB).

Life Application: When your faith is under fire, it is important to remember that fire is what God uses to make your faith flourish.

JUNE 4

Life is too short to be so serious all the time.
Life Application: Smile often; play more; sing more; dance more. Just live!

JUNE 5

The Lord is a refuge for the oppressed, a stronghold in the times of trouble - Psalms 9:9 (NIV).

Life Application: When the storms rage, my soul will rest in God's embrace.

JUNE 6

Believe God to always turn your mess into a beautiful message.

Life Application: He is the God of beautiful endings; just trust Him.

JUNE 7

Because the sovereign Lord helps me, I will not be disgraced. Therefore, I have set my face like a stone determined to do His will. And I know that I will not be put to shame - Isaiah 50:7.

Life Application: Trusting God is everything you need to survive.

JUNE 8

Your confidence in God will produce His manifestation in your life.

Life Application: Do you remember Elijah and the prophets of Baal? If you trust God, He will manifest on your behalf, just as he did for Elijah.

JUNE 9

There are a lot of possibilities in dis-abilities.

Life Application: All it takes is changing your perspective.

JUNE 10

Do not allow temporary challenges to take you away from your place of opportunity.

Life Application: A life of shortcuts and ease will give you results far less than what you will get if you live out the challenges and wait full term, for the results.

JUNE 11

For we know, that all things work together for good, to them that love God - Romans 8:28 (KJV).

Life Application: God will not waste your pain; rather, He will turn your pain into a gain.

JUNE 12

Success in life is an inside job.

Life Application: To be successful, you have to believe within you that anything is possible.

JUNE 13

To whom much is given, much is expected.

Life Application: Your uniqueness is not a virtue; it is a responsibility, and it requires accountability to the One who designed your destiny.

JUNE 14

When the purpose of a thing is not known, abuse is inevitable.

Life Application: The joy of discovery helps you to find out who you are and liberates you from what you are not.

JUNE 15

If the founder of Kentucky Fried Chicken (KFC) could discover his purpose in his 60s, then discovering yours now, irrespective of age, is not such a bad idea.

Life Application: Do not believe the lies of the enemy; it is never too late to be who you might have been earlier.

JUNE 16

Self-discovery reality check: Are you making a living or are you making a life?

Life Application: What matters most on your death bed are the lives you impacted. They live on to spread your legacy. Live wisely.

JUNE 17

Discovery precedes purpose.

Life Application: When you find your true identity, you find your true purpose.

JUNE 18

Time is measured in minutes, but life is measured in moments.

Life Application: Enjoy your life, the memories matter.

JUNE 19

Every past experience, whether good or bad, is preparation for some future opportunity.

Life Application: See every experience as a teaching tool; identify your lessons and keep them for future reference.

JUNE 20

You are beautifully and wonderfully made in God's image.

Life Application: To see yourself as anything other than God's masterpiece is to devalue and distort your true identity - Matt Batterson.

JUNE 21

When your life is over, the world will ask only one question: "Did you do what you were supposed to do?" - Korczak Ziolkowski.

Life Application: In essence, make your life count.

JUNE 22

What a person can become, he or she must become or be miserable.

Life Application: Choose to become what you were created for so as not to live the rest of your life with regrets.

JUNE 23

Successful individuals have one secret in common; they leverage their weaknesses by discovering new strengths.

Life Application: Always see new challenges as a means to learn and grow.

JUNE 24

You teach what you know, but you reproduce who you are - Wayne Cordiero.

Life Application: In the natural order of life, an orange tree cannot bear apples. So it is with life; your prevalent thoughts are a reflection of who you are.

JUNE 25

When a proud sheep chooses to live the life of a lion, just the roar of the lion pack will send him running - African Proverb.

Life Application: The deepest form of despair is to choose to be someone other than oneself (Soren Kierkegaard). Remember that your value is hidden in your uniqueness.

JUNE 26

Faith is the thumbprint that logs you into God's grace - Levi Lusko.

Life Application: Faith helps us to make sense of God's grace, which we usually do not deserve.

JUNE 27

"Impossible," is just a big word thrown around by small men who find it easier to live in the world they have been given, than to explore the power they have to change it - Adidas.

Life Application: Developing a mindset that everything is possible is the key to great achievements.

JUNE 28

There is a God-shaped vacuum in the heart of every man which cannot be filled by any created thing, but only by God, the Creator, made known through Jesus Christ - Blaise Pascal.

Life Application: The true meaning of life is found is connecting with the God of the universe.

JUNE 29

You have made us for yourself, O Lord; our hearts are restless until they rest in you - Saint Augustine.

Life Application: Futility of life is in assuming ownership of your life.

JUNE 30

God is greater than your past, present and future combined.

Life Application: Are you on a guilt trip? Do you feel you are not worth it? Joy Alert; your true value is in God's acceptance of you.

JULY

JULY 1

"Impossible" does not only rob you of your future, it also deprives you of enjoying the present moment of your life.

Life Application: Do not let the words "It is not possible," rob you of awesome and amazing outcomes. The least result of your efforts is a negative response or a discontinued project. In the end, you can rest assured that you tried.

JULY 2

Vision without action is a daydream. Action without vision is a nightmare - Japanese Proverb.

Life Application: First, Vision; then, Action. They work together.

JULY 3

Die empty! - Dr. Myles Munroe.

Life Application: Graveyards are filled with all manner of potential that remained potential. What a tragedy! Make your life count today.

JULY 4

The only limitation in your life is the one you set for yourself.

Life Application: If you want to be successful, finish your victory in your mind, and envision its reality.

JULY 5

You cannot wash the feet of a dirty world if you refuse to touch it - Erwin McManus.

Life Application: Compassion is all you need in life to bring people out from what ails them.

JULY 6

Your biggest disability in life is your bad attitude.

Life Application: People will always remember you more for your attitude, than for your possessions.

JULY 7

The best way to do something is to quit talking about it and start doing it.

Life Application: Take Action now!

JULY 8

It is not what you were that matters, but what you can become.

Life Application: Strive to become better every day of your life

JULY 9

God never promised you a trouble-free life of leisure, but He does promise that He will never leave you and will always love you.

Life Application: God is bigger than any trouble that will confront you.

JULY 10

When you know who you are and grow into your purpose, God revises the way you see the future.

Life Application: The key to a better future is finding the reason for your existence.

JULY 11

You are not a collection of labels glued together by your acceptance of other people's perception of you.

Life Application: What you think about yourself is more important than what others think of you.

JULY 12

Aspire to do something great today.

Life Application: Greatness starts the moment you wake up.

JULY 13

Have a blessed day or make it a great day. Which one is better? The choice is yours and mine.

Life Application: The ability to choose is a very powerful force in life.

JULY 14

To lead others well, you must first lead yourself - Jenni Catron.

Life Application: Every true leader embraces the principle of self-discipline.

JULY 15

A qualified apology is the trademark of a prideful heart.

Life Application: Apology and pride do not mesh. If you are sorry for your actions, mean it.

JULY 16

There is a law for confession; you just say what God has said.

Life Application: Your words are very powerful.

JULY 17

Quit living as if the purpose of life is to arrive safely at death - Matt Batterson.

Life Application: The real deal about living is not staying safe. It is about taking risks and living life to the fullest, with divine wisdom.

July 18

Do not let what is wrong with you keep you from what is right with God. Worship Him.

Life Application: God is greater than your mistakes.

July 19

Quit complaining about what is wrong; start doing something that makes a difference.

Life Application: Focus on what you can change.

July 20

Only those who will risk going too far can possibly find out how far one can go - T.S. Elliot.

Life Application: You are one idea, one risk, and one decision away from a totally different life.

July 21

Courage is not the absence of fear; courage is triumph over fear. The brave man is not he who does not feel afraid, but he who conquers that fear - Nelson Mandela.

Life Application: You will continue to run for the rest of your life, unless you confront that which makes you afraid.

July 22

Never give up on something you really want to achieve. Yes, it may be difficult because of fear, but even worse is to be full of regrets. Be bold!

Life Application: Do not forfeit your dreams on the altar of fear.

JULY 23

Do yourself a big favor; allow God to get between you and your circumstances.

Life Application: God uses the circumstances of our lives as a springboard for our future successes.

JULY 24

God's dream for your life is so much bigger and so much better than simply breaking even.

Life Application: Living a life of purpose is much more than earning a living.

JULY 25

God honors big dreams because big dreams honor God.

Life Application: If your prayers are not impossible to you, they are insults to God.

JULY 26

The best way to discover your God ordained destiny is to help other people accomplish their dreams.

Life Application: It is in helping others that we find ourselves.

JULY 27

If other people's joy makes you feel uncomfortable, your faith is questionable.

Life Application: You know successful people by their genuine happiness for other people's progress.

JULY 28

When you are not secure in your identity, you waste much of your time trying to fulfill the unrealistic expectations that others have placed on you.

Life Application: Identity is purpose. When you discover who you are, everyone else's opinions will be baseless to you.

JULY 29

The size of your dream is the accurate measure of the size of your God.

Life Application: No matter how big your righteous dream is, God can bring it to pass. And He will!

JULY 30

Imagination is God's gift to you; a dream is your gift back to God - Matt Batterson.

Life Application: Imagine, dream, and be what God has called you to be.

JULY 31

Your greatest legacy in life is not your dream; your greatest legacy is the next generation of dreamers that your dream inspires.

Life Application: Who will benefit from your story? If this is your question, trust me, they will come.

AUGUST

AUGUST 1

An act of kindness can make a world of difference to one person today.

Life Application: Kindness is one of the cheapest lifelong products in the world.

AUGUST 2

As I walked out of the door toward the gate that would lead to my freedom, I knew if I did not leave my bitterness and hatred behind, I would still be in prison - Nelson Mandela.

Life Application: When you choose to forgive, you set yourself free.

AUGUST 3

Make every effort to stay away from negative people; they have a problem for every good solution.

Life Application: If you end a conversation with a friend or colleague and you feel sad, it is a sign for you to scale back on your interactions with them.

AUGUST 4

The true measure of a person's character is what the person would do if the person knew he or she would never be found out.

Life Application: Being called a good man or a good woman should mean that you would still be good, when there are no cameras or people around.

AUGUST 5

Do not allow other people to hold the key to your peace of mind.

Life Application: You can be happy; own it!

AUGUST 6

When it hurts to look back and it is scary to look ahead, look up and find God; He will always be there for you.

Life Application: God is Alpha and Omega; trust Him.

AUGUST 7

Send the weapon of faith to answer the door when fear comes knocking.

Life Application: Every problem has a solution. For fear, the solution is faith. And to get faith, you must read and hear more of God's word.

AUGUST 8

So we fix our eyes not on what is seen but on what is unseen. For what is seen is temporary, but what is unseen is eternal - 2 Corinthians 4:18 (NIV).

Life Application: Do not allow immediate challenges to rob you of future glory.

AUGUST 9

Stop focusing on how stressed and depressed you are; start focusing on how blessed you are.

Life Application: What you focus on the most is what you magnify. Begin to practice opposing your negative thoughts. For every feeling of sadness, think joy.

AUGUST 10

Do not strive to become who others want you to be, but who God made you to be.

Life Application: Imitation is limitation. Be You.

AUGUST 11

The only limit to prayer is how limited it is in our lives - Jentezen Franklin.

Life Application: Pray without ceasing.

AUGUST 12

For I know the plans I have for you, declares the Lord, plans to prosper you and not to harm you; plans to give you hope and a future - Jeremiah 29:11 (NIV).

Life Application: There is no one on earth who can love you and keep you like God can. Let Him be your choice, always.

AUGUST 13

Limitations persist until God ends every evil plan against your destiny.

Life Application: When God steps in, problems have no choice but to fall out.

AUGUST 14

Life is not about waiting for the storm to pass; it is about learning to dance in the rain.

Life Application: I was once someone who runs away from challenges...until I realized that facing them felt like being the lead actor in a blockbuster movie.

AUGUST 15

Resentment is like drinking poison and then hoping it will kill your enemies – Nelson Mandela.

Life Application: Forgiveness is for you, not the other person. Forgiveness makes you productive.

AUGUST 16

Obedience always leads to blessings; disobedience always leads to curses. This is an all-time principle.

Life Application: Every action has positive or negative consequences.

AUGUST 17

The brave man is not he who does not feel afraid, but he who conquers that fear - Nelson Mandela.

Life Application: Fear is normal, but would you let it cripple you?

AUGUST 18

You cannot make demands until you are in demand – T. D. Jakes.

Life Application: When you give or provide value, you give credence to the value you place on yourself.

AUGUST 19

You cannot contribute to the success of what is designed to destroy you, and still expect to be delivered from it.

Life Application: Do not tolerate what could ultimately destroy you.

AUGUST 20

The most important part of any building, person, or plan, is the foundation.

Life Application: The foundation is the least visible but the most necessary.

AUGUST 21

Do not be too preoccupied with life's provisions, instead of its purpose.

Life Application: The glory of living is when it is impactful.

AUGUST 22

Life is an adventure which only the strong survive.

Life Application: Courage and determination are two keys for a successful life.

AUGUST 23

It is the condition of your heart, not your personality, that attracts the favor of God to your life.

Life Application: Life is not measured by what we do but by the intentions that drive us.

AUGUST 24

God always gives us a way to escape when we are tempted; the key is to slow down - Levi Lusko.

Life Application: Always anticipate the consequences of your decisions.

AUGUST 25

True friends are like jewels; precious and rare. Fake friends are like autumn leaves; found everywhere - Ari Joseph.

Life Application: If you have true friends, hold onto them.

AUGUST 26

Anxiety does not empty tomorrow of its sorrows, but only empties today of its strength – Charles Spurgeon.

Life Application: Always keep a happy attitude, no matter the circumstances in life.

AUGUST 27

Restoration is God giving you what is best now, instead of what was better, then - Dr. Anthonia Adeyeye.

Life Application: Do not settle for leftovers. Ask for the best.

AUGUST 28

When you live for self, you end up on the shelf, good for nothing - Dr. Festus Adeyeye.

Life Application: Life is valuable when it adds value to others.

AUGUST 29

We are never ready; however, the only chance that we have to rise to our true destiny is when we rise to the challenges that life throws at us – Author Unknown.

Life Application: The best time to live is now. Like the Nike slogan, "Just Do It."

AUGUST 30

Do not compare your life with others; you have no clue what their journey is all about.

Life Application: Comparison brings frustration in life.

AUGUST 31

Do not criticize what you cannot understand - Bob Dylan.

Life Application: Always seek to know before you assume.

SEPTEMBER

SEPTEMBER 1

Wake up every day expecting that miracles like raindrops await you, wherever you go.

Life Application: The thoughts of your heart become your reality. If you program your mind to be expectant, you will receive.

SEPTEMBER 2

Success is like pregnancy; everybody congratulates you, but not everyone knows how many times you failed to conceive.

Life Application: Whatever it is you do, irrespective of how people perceive your dream, keep at it; one day, it will speak.

SEPTEMBER 3

The Heavenly Hand that points the way is the same hand that provides the way – Author Unknown.

Life Application: How you identify a God-given purpose is that there will always be provision along the way. So rest easy, God has got you covered.

SEPTEMBER 4

You cannot live and strive outside of what God created you to be.
Life Application: Maximize your innate talents and giftings.

SEPTEMBER 5

Do not base your identity on things you can lose - Dr. Festus Adeyeye.

Life Application: The things that matter the most in life are not material, because material things fade away, but God is eternal. Choose God, always.

SEPTEMBER 6

One of the biggest ways we misuse our time is not knowing where we are going next.

Life Application: Planning is very important. Never overlook this stage.

SEPTEMBER 7

At any moment of our lives, we are either choosing to acknowledge the blessings we have been given or complaining about those we have not yet received.

Life Application: Cultivate a lifestyle of thanksgiving. Be grateful that you are alive; that you can walk; that you can eat; and that you can read this book. Gratitude makes room for more blessings.

SEPTEMBER 8

It is not enough to admit your inadequacies; it is better you resolve them.

Life Application: Growth is first admitting that you are wrong, and second, turning a new leaf entirely.

SEPTEMBER 9

Every wrong belief leads to wrong behavior.

Life Application: I do not believe that bad things just happen. First, there is always a thought. Watch your thoughts

SEPTEMBER 10

You may not know why you must wait, but you can believe and trust that God knows what He is doing.

Life Application: God is never late; trust Him.

SEPTEMBER 11

Guard your character; it is your most valuable asset in life.

Life Application: People remember you not for what you have or who you are, but mostly for how you make them feel - Maya Angelou.

SEPTEMBER 12

What will be does not have to be when you make the right choices in life.

Life Application: Life does not happen by accident. Be purposeful.

SEPTEMBER 13

While you are alive, collect moments, not things; earn respect, not money; and enjoy love, not luxuries - Aarti Khurana.

Life Application: The greatest return on investment in life is happiness, and material things do not bring lasting happiness.

SEPTEMBER 14

Do not break your faith before your breakthrough.

Life Application: Faith can be hard, but if you keep holding on to what you believe will happen, it will happen.

SEPTEMBER 15

And Jesus said, "if any would be great among you, he must first become a servant" - Matthew 23:11 (Paraphrased).

Life Application: You only receive value from life when you give value to others.

SEPTEMBER 16

"Be fruitful and multiply," was not a suggestion from God, but an expectation backed by a divine command.

Life Application: As humans, one of our major attributes is the capacity to reproduce. As such, whether in our businesses, careers, or family lives, we must expect to increase/expand and develop/grow.

SEPTEMBER 17

When you choose to trust in God's care in spite of your fears, He will equip you for moving forward in His blessings.

Life Application: Would it not be better to trust the One who owns the whole world? You are protected when you trust in Him.

SEPTEMBER 18

Guard your heart above all else, for it determines the course of your life – Proverbs 4:23.

Life Application: Do not entertain fear and doubt. The moment you do, they steal your peace.

SEPTEMBER 19

Just because some people dress better than you, for example, does not mean that they are indeed better than you.

Life Application: Contentment and self-love are virtues that will keep you from comparing yourself with others.

SEPTEMBER 20

Life is a matter of choices and every choice you make, makes you - John C. Maxwell.

Life Application: The very next choice we will make determines whether we are on the path towards victory or defeat.

SEPTEMBER 21

Whenever you say "Yes" to something, less of you is available for something else. Make sure your "Yes" is worth the "less of you."

Life Application: Always strive to make the right choices in life.

SEPTEMBER 22

Nothing else matters, nothing in this world will do; Jesus, You are the center, and everything revolves around You... - "Jesus at the Center," by Israel and the New Breed.

Life Application: Your total perception of yourself will melt away when you know Jesus as your Savior.

SEPTEMBER 23

Whoever you choose to do life with will ultimately determine the outcome of your life.

Life Application: Choose the people you allow to influence your life, wisely.

SEPTEMBER 24

You cannot prevent birds of sorrow from flying over your head, but you can prevent them from building nests in your hair - Chinese Proverb.

Life Application: The power to stay happy or sad lies with you.

SEPTEMBER 25

Our feelings are real, and they are powerful; but they should not be the dictators of our actions.

Life Application: Feelings are like waves; they rise and fall. An action you take based on a feeling may be regretted later.

SEPTEMBER 26

When God gave us the capacity to control our thoughts, He gave us a powerful ability. We have the ability to cheer ourselves up no matter what our circumstances are - Joyce Meyer.

Life Application: Take personal responsibility for the daily outcomes of your life.

SEPTEMBER 27

Whatever you say, say it on purpose; whatever you do, do it on purpose.

Life Application: Be intentional and deliberate in whatever you do.

SEPTEMBER 28

For you to be victorious in the battle of life, the level of your faith and your determination must be greater than the challenges confronting you.

Life Application: Cultivate the art of focused determination.

SEPTEMBER 29

Your enemy says you cannot go far, but God says you can go far and beyond.

Life Application: The finality of your life is determined by God

SEPTEMBER 30

Whatever you do not demand, you cannot command - Dr. Festus Adeyeye.

Life Application: You cannot possess what you do not seek.

OCTOBER

OCTOBER 1

Our reaction to a situation literally has the power to change the situation itself.

Life Application: You may not be responsible for every event in your life, but your response-ability will determine the outcome of your destiny.

OCTOBER 2

Teamwork: Achieving more, together.

Life Application: If you want to go far and fast in life, you need a good team.

OCTOBER 3

When God builds your life, nothing can hinder you.

Life Application: People see God with the same eyes with which they see men. God is not like man and when you have His backing, you are settled.

OCTOBER 4

Sometimes, what appears to be a setback is God's mode of elevation.

Life Application: Potential setback and difficulties are sometimes stepping stones to our next dimension in life.

OCTOBER 5

Change your life today. Do not gamble on the future; act now without delay - Simone de Beauvoir.

Life Application: Your present-tense action has a future-tense ramification.

OCTOBER 6

You have to fight to achieve your dream. You have to sacrifice and work hard for it.

Life Application: The true assessment of a gift is what you are willing to give up for receiving it.

OCTOBER 7

If we are unfaithful, He remains faithful, for He cannot deny who He is - 2 Timothy 2:13.

Life Application: You cannot overdraw on God's faithfulness. This is a valid statement, for all time.

OCTOBER 8

But by the grace of God, I am what I am, and His grace towards me was not in vain - 1 Cor. 15:10 (NKJV).

Life Application: When you step out of God's grace, you start expiring.

OCTOBER 9

The mystery of human existence lies not just in staying alive, but in finding something to live for - Fyodor Dostoyevsky.

Life Application: You start living a life of purpose, the day you discover a dream worth dying for.

OCTOBER 10

I have been crucified with Christ, and it is no longer I who live, but Christ lives in me; and the life which I now live in the flesh I live by faith in the son of God, who loved me and gave Himself up for me – Galatians 2:20 (NASB).

Life Application: You begin to live fully when your heart stops beating for the things that break the heart of God.

OCTOBER 11

One of my greatest fears is the thought of going through life without seeing God show Himself powerfully on my behalf.

Life Application: Supernatural living is the cure for an average life.

OCTOBER 12

The tongue can bring death or life; those who love to talk will reap the consequences - Proverbs 18:21.

Life Application: Do not underestimate the power of spoken affirmation, for it has the potential to change a person's life.

OCTOBER 13

You rob God of the opportunity to do something supernatural when you avoid difficult situations of life.

Life Application: You should never pray not to have troubles; rather, you should pray for God to give you the wisdom and grace to overcome. Your testimonies are tales of encouragement to others.

OCTOBER 14

Life is not about finding the answers; it is about asking the questions - Brian Grazer.

Life Application: Perfect the art of developing and asking the right and most appropriate questions that will generate enlightening and favorable answers. Awaken your curiosity.

OCTOBER 15

King Solomon offered a sacrifice of 22,000 oxen and 120,000 sheep. So the king and all the people dedicated the house of God - 2 Chronicles 7:5 (ESV).

Life Application: Try giving beyond your means if you want God to do something beyond your ability.

OCTOBER 16

You miss divine miracles when you ignore divine prompting.

Life Application: As long as you have a relationship with God and you study His word, be in the habit of obeying the instructions you receive in your spirit.

OCTOBER 17

Divine opportunity does not make appointments; it usually shows up at your doorstep unannounced.

Life Application: Most folks call blessings, "luck." I call them divine opportunities that meet me prepared. So whatever it is you do, do it well, so that you never miss divine opportunities.

OCTOBER 18

Your inaction today can cost you your tomorrow.

Life Application: The Holy Spirit does a lot of prompting. He prompts you to take courses, make investments, or go to certain places. I never regret taking any of those actions.

OCTOBER 19

Do not let what you cannot accomplish today deprive you of doing what you can accomplish tomorrow.

Life Application: I once had nothing in my life, and I began forming the habit of believing that since I did not have the resources presently, I would not be able to achieve certain goals in the future. Thank God for spiritual growth and the blessings of faith! No matter your present lack, there must be a conviction in you that tomorrow will be better.

OCTOBER 20

The Mighty One, God, our Lord, speaks and summons the earth from the rising of the sun to where it sets - Psalm 50: 1 (NIV).

Life Application: If you know whose son or daughter you are, you will never be afraid.

OCTOBER 21

You cannot judge a promise or a disappointment by its cover.

Life Application: The best gift anyone can receive in this dispensation is the gift of discernment.

OCTOBER 22

We are deceived whenever we think that we have a better plan for our lives than God does.

Life Application: You may acquire whatever it is you need in life, but peace is something you cannot buy. Peace comes from God.

OCTOBER 23

Anything outside of God's good is the wrong "good" thing.

Life Application: Do not substitute best for good.

OCTOBER 24

When you are knocked down, do not stay down.

Life Application: Failure is temporary; success is achieved when you refuse to give up.

☙❧

OCTOBER 25

Do not focus on finding the right person; focus on becoming the right person.

Life Application: A lot of times we are tricked into believing that we can find the one we love just the way we are. My take on this is that you should make a list of what you want in a partner, and then live your life in such a manner that when you meet, you complement him or her.

OCTOBER 26

God wants you to get where He wants you to go, more than you want to get where God wants you to go - Matt Batterson.

Life Application: God wants you to succeed, but to do so, you have to agree and partner with Him.

OCTOBER 27

Enjoy the Journey – T. D. Jakes.

Life Application: Stop focusing all your energy on the next season of your life; enjoy the season you are in right now.

OCTOBER 28

The further backward you look; the further forward you are likely to see - Winston Churchill.

Life Application: Those who fail to learn from history are bound to make the same mistakes.

OCTOBER 29

I believe that God uses the wind of circumstances to change the projection of our lives.

Life Application: Great endings will result from whatever you are going through today, no matter how bad it is.

OCTOBER 30

If you choose not to deal with an issue, then you give up your right of control over the issue, and it will select the path of least resistance - Susan Del Gatto.

Life Application: You cannot solve a problem when you do not recognize or acknowledge it.

OCTOBER 31

It is neither the law of religion nor the principles of morality that define our highways and pathways to God; only by the Grace of God are we led and drawn to Him. It is His grace that conquers a multitude of flaws and in that grace, there is only favor. As C. JoyBell C. said, "Favor is not achieved; favor is received."

Life Application: Thank God for G. R. A. C. E.; God's Riches At Christ's Expense.

NOVEMBER

NOVEMBER 1

For the scriptures tell us, "Abraham believed God, and God counted him as righteous because of his faith" - Romans 4:3.

Life Application: God is not looking for your extraordinary ability; He desires your fearless obedience.

NOVEMBER 2

Success is not final, and failure is not fatal. It is the courage to continue that counts.

Life Application: It is okay not to be okay, if you do not give up.

NOVEMBER 3

Again, I say to you, that if two of you shall agree on the earth concerning any matter, whatsoever it may be that they shall ask, it shall come to them from my Father who is in the heavens – Matthew 18:19 (DBT).

Life Application: It takes two to tango, and it takes two to conquer. Never underestimate the power of unity.

NOVEMBER 4

Your breakthrough from any situation comes by the revelation of the word. Breakthrough is achieved when a powerful, evil, and ruling presence over a territory has been destroyed.

Life Application: Today, let your prayer be for God to give you a word for every situation you encounter.

NOVEMBER 5

According to an African proverb, when there is no enemy within, the enemy outside can do you no harm.

Life Application: Your mindset is both your worst enemy and your best friend.

NOVEMBER 6

A gentle answer turns away wrath, but a harsh word, stirs up anger - Proverbs 15: 1 (NIV).

Life Application: Gentleness is the best prescription for roughness - Levi Lusko.

NOVEMBER 7

When God does not make sense...

Life Application: ...Do not try to understand God; rather, take a step of faith to trust Him.

NOVEMBER 8

For we know that all things (whether good or bad) work together for good to them that love God, to those who are called according to his purpose - Romans 8:28 (KJV).

Life Application: The truth of the Cross of Jesus Christ is simple; only God can use our wrong choices to bring us to the right places.

NOVEMBER 9

People may not remember exactly what you did or what you said, but they will always remember how you made them feel - Maya Angelou.

Life Application: Make it a point of duty to ensure that anyone who leaves you, leaves you feeling better than before they met you.

NOVEMBER 10

The further you get away from yourself, the more challenging it is... - Benedict Cumberbatch.

Life Application: Do not be so tempted by your present luxury and material possessions, that you abandon the greater purpose for which you were born.

NOVEMBER 11

Your vision may be real to you, but you cannot get to tomorrow while you are wrestling with today - T.D. Jakes.

Life Application: Do not allow your past to rob you of a great future.

NOVEMBER 12

Focus your energy on what you should be doing instead of what you want to stop doing.

Life Application: Life teaches us that if we want to be better people, we have to deal with our flaws. As such, people focus so much on doing the right thing and become depressed when they fail. You must learn to magnify your strengths and minimize your weaknesses.

NOVEMBER 13

If you want to soar high, you will have to give up the issues that weigh you down.

Life Application: Picture yourself trying to climb 200 flights of stairs. In each hand, you have two heavy duffel bags, and on your back, you have a military-style rucksack. Practically speaking, making progress will be difficult. So it is with life; the more you focus on self-hate, self-loathing, anger and jealousy, the more stagnant you will be.

NOVEMBER 14

Be careful what you ask for; you will get it.

Life Application: Asking is believing and believing produces results.

NOVEMBER 15

Be it unto you according to your faith - Mathew 9:29 (KJV).

Life Application: Faith is not an argument, it is a choice; it is not a debate, it is a decision.

NOVEMBER 16

For He says, "In a favorable time I listened to you, and in a day of salvation I have helped you. Behold, now is the favorable time; behold now is the day of salvation" - 2 Cor. 6:2 (ESV).

Life Application: God has no time limits; yet, He does have a favorite time; and that time is now.

NOVEMBER 17

But do not forget this one thing, dear friends: with the Lord, a day is like a thousand years, and a thousand years are like a day – 2 Peter 3:8 (NIV).

Life Application: With God, it is not too late, and it has never been too late.

NOVEMBER 18

If you are born poor it is not your mistake, but if you die poor it is your mistake - Bill Gates.

Life Application: Your present situation is not the outcome you must accept. Always strive to be and do better.

NOVEMBER 19

It is dangerous to look at yourself and see a long-past expiration date.

Life Application: If you see yourself as great, you will be great. If you see yourself as poor, weak and wretched, that is what you will become. Choose to believe what God says about you.

NOVEMBER 20

By His grace, and by nothing you can offer, God accepts you.

Life Application: The invitation is "come unto me all ye that labor and a heavy laden…" The invitation is "Come."

NOVEMBER 21

The greatest commandment is that you love your neighbor as yourself.

Life Application: When you live in the world called, "self-everything," you cut yourself from the things only God can offer. Love makes you give of yourself to others, and in return, you will be blessed.

NOVEMBER 22

Integrity, reputation, and honesty have greater value than money alone.

Life Application: Strive to be credible, instead of being incredible.

NOVEMBER 23

"I have known the father cares for me, He's been good, He's been good. Through it all, He is always there for me; God's been good to me. Through the storm, through the night, come what may, everything is going to be alright. I have known the father cares for me, He's been good to me…" - Lyrics from Ron Kenoly's "He's Been Good."

Life Application: God cares for you so much that you can trust Him when you are going through hard times.

NOVEMBER 24

The rich rule over the poor, and the borrower is slave to the lender - Proverbs 22:7 (NIV).

Life Application: You cannot negotiate with a tiger when your head is in its mouth - Winston Churchill.

NOVEMBER 25

Give a man a fish and you feed him for a day; teach him how to fish and you feed him for a lifetime.

Life Application: The true leader is one who leads people while teaching them to be independent. If you have such an opportunity, make it happen; liberate people.

NOVEMBER 26

It is easy to smile and sing when there is nothing to bring you down.

Life Application: Pressures of life reveal your true character.

NOVEMBER 27

If I am wrong about God, then I wasted my life. It you are wrong about God, then you wasted your eternity – Lecrae.

Life Application: God is real; do not let anyone tell you a lie; do not let circumstances tell you otherwise.

NOVEMBER 28

But just as He who called you is holy, so be holy in all you do - 1 Peter 1:15 (NIV).

Life Application: God did not create you to be happy; He created you to be holy.

NOVEMBER 29

When everything is awesome, we may miss what (and who) is truly deserving of awe – Kevin DeYoung.

Life Application: The glory should always be given to God, for He is truly awesome.

For every choice you want to make, sit back and think. You may realize that what you so desperately want may not be a priority at that moment.

Life Application: That the change you desperately crave may not be the change you want, is a fundamental truth in life.

DECEMBER

DECEMBER 1

Fulfilling purpose is the best thing you can do for yourself and for generations after you.

Life Application: God intended for you to fulfill a purpose and not to be a superwoman or superman.

DECEMBER 2

When the good people in a society decide to keep quiet, people suffer and die.

Life Application: It is not enough to be willing to do the right thing; you must be ready to teach and encourage other people to do the right thing.

DECEMBER 3

Habits beget character and character begets destiny.

Life Application: The way you do little things will ultimately be the way you do everything.

DECEMBER 4

For just as the heavens are higher hat the earth, so my ways are higher than your ways and my thoughts higher than your thoughts – Isaiah 55:8-9.

Life Application: My feelings are not God; God is God. My feelings do not define truth; God's word defines truth - John Piper.

DECEMBER 5

Wasted potential is when one's natural giftedness lacks a complementary work ethic.

Life Application: If the place you find yourself is not pushing you mentally, then it is time for you to leave, to act upon your potential

December 6

No one achieves his or her dream by wishful thinking.

Life Application: You have everything it takes to achieve any dream in life, but you cannot, if you sit and do nothing. Actions bring dreams to reality.

December 7

God gave us emotions so we could more deeply experience life but not destroy life - Lysa Terkeurst.

Life Application: Your emotions were never designed to direct the outcomes of your life.

December 8

The way you make your bed is the way you lie on it.

Life Application: The decisions you make today will determine the stories you will tell about your life tomorrow.

December 9

It is the direction you follow and not the intention you have, that will determine your destination.

Life Application: Intention without action does not produce any result.

December 10

Live a life that does not make sense when you are away from God.

Life Application: Whatsoever therefore you eat, or drink, or whatsoever you do, do all to the glory of God - 1 Cor. 10:31.

DECEMBER 11

Trust in the Lord with all your heart, and lean not on thine own understanding. In all your ways acknowledge him, and he shall direct your paths. Proverbs 3: 5-6 (KJV).

Life Application: When you are unclear about what God is doing in your life, you will fall prey to outsiders' views of the situation.

DECEMBER 12

Here is something you must understand about God's love. It is as strong as we are fragile, and His patience is more powerful than our failures.

Life Application: Everything you see as an imperfection in your life is totally absent in God. Yet, He loves you. This knowledge should help you to overcome self-loathing or self-pity.

DECEMBER 13

God cares for you deeply, but He is never thinking of you alone. His plans are always bigger than you and that is for your ultimate good.

Life Application: God has said that He loves you. He is not one to mince words; trust Him, and always have it in mind that He wants the best for you.

DECEMBER 14

Your perspective of your current situation can either encourage or dampen your trust in your God.

Life Application: Let the word of God be made flesh in your spirit, so that no matter what comes your way, your trust in God does not waver.

DECEMBER 15

A winning lifestyle is not an accident.

Life Application: Life by design does not just happen; it is deliberately calculated and intended, by those who embrace it.

DECEMBER 16

Ask not what God can do for you; rather, ask God what you can do for Him.

Life Application: That which you desire from God becomes easily attainable when your primary focus is to do the Lord's Will.

DECEMBER 17

It is better to act on life than to simply allow life to act on you.

Life Application: Stop making excuses. Start taking action.

DECEMBER 18

Yesterday's decisions are the stories you will tell today; today's decisions are the stories you will tell tomorrow.

Life Application: Decisions are part and parcel of life, so carefully and intentionally make wise decisions.

DECEMBER 19

Tell yourself: "Just for today, I will focus on recovering, loving and enjoying life."

Life Application: Many people postpone their joy for tomorrow, when they can start enjoying life today, despite the challenges it brings.

DECEMBER 20

A person that does not heed advice will find that sooner or later, he is surrounded by people who have nothing to say.

Life Application: You are a sum total of everything you hear. Listen wisely.

DECEMBER 21

You do not just let the future happen; you make it happen with God's help.

Life Application: Life is for the living and not for waiting around. There is an expected future if it is established by instrumental steps.

DECEMBER 22

Trust in the Lord God always, for in the Lord Jehovah is everlasting strength - Isaiah 26:4 (LB).

Life Application: Stress says it must be done now; faith says trust in God.

DECEMBER 23

Your life is not defined by the multitude of problems; it is defined by your commitment to overcome these problems.

Life Application: Life is full of challenges; however, the glory of successful living is one's ability to overcome the challenges of life.

DECEMBER 24

"Impossible," does not exist in God's vocabulary.

Life Application: One lesson I learned from the docu-series, "The Men who built America," is that they believed that anything is possible. If you are full of doubts, make room for possibilities.

DECEMBER 25

"Impossible," is another word for an excuse not to try.

Life Application: Never say it cannot be done unless you have attempted it.

DECEMBER 26

Everyone has something in his or her hands; unfortunately, not everyone recognizes and appreciates the value of what they have.

Life Application: The beauty of life is that everyone has something to give, whether big or small.

December 27

"Positive anything" is better than "negative nothing" - Author Unknown.

Life Application: Which is better? To have a poorly paid job or no job at all? People waste precious time daydreaming about their ideal job rather than doing what is available.

December 28

We cannot solve our problems with the same mindset we had when we created them.

Life Application: In the course of interacting with people from various spheres of life, I come across two sets of people; those who solve problems by creating new problems, and those who solve problems by creating solutions.

December 29

The pursuit of being significant is far greater than the pursuit of being successful.

Life Application: Life is about impacting others to succeed and to realize their true potential.

December 30

Trust in the Lord with all your heart, and lean not on your own understanding - Proverbs 3:5 (NKJV).

Life Application: Faith means trusting God absolutely, without a second thought that He cannot do it.

December 31

I press on toward the goal to win the prize for which God has called me heavenward in Christ Jesus - Philippians 3: 14 (NIV).

Life Application: Life is about moving forward and not looking back at disappointments. A car that is in reverse mode will not move forward, and the same is true for our lives.

Made in the USA
Monee, IL
26 January 2021